Being creative with Software through the Ages

Two Decades of Developing and Using Computer Programs

Clemens Willemsen PhD

ISBN: 979-88-0122-128-1
Printed and published by: Kindle Direct Publishing
Copyright: Clemens Willemsen 2023

Table of contents

List of Figures

List of Tables

List of Attachments

Att. 1. Your own software and programs through the ages

1. Introduction

How have software and programs evolved over the years and helped us to do our work more efficiently or used for fun at leisure times? You might have acquired a new program, read the user manual with the diagram of possible features and wonder what it all means. This book is about my personal experience with software and programming.
Two decades is the period I take into account from around the 1980's to the 2000's where I start my story with MS Dos as an example and end with Open office as an example. I will look a little further at new developments in recent decades as well though. I will explain how I see the forces behind these developments and where I can, I will add 'proof' from literature and research on these subjects[1]. What can we learn from the past and predict for the future? I have been interested in this matter ever since I used my first computer program. The programs I mention in this book are mostly the ones I have used in the past privately or for work.

In my book of 2022 'Connecting Consumer Devices through the Ages' I look back at 70 years of consumer devices and mostly the hardware that was used for computers. I do not have that long of a history for working with computers myself but I look back at using software and programming for two decades. I have done so as a student, privately and professionally and want to show you what programs I used in those days and what I programmed. Mostly this was during my university studies between 1979 and 1985 and professionally between 1985 and 1998. So the subtitle of this book could be related to my two previous books as 'Two decades of software and programming'.

As a student in those days there were not many options on computers. Programming took place with punch cards in languages as Fortran, Pascal and Cobol when only minutes later you would receive the result on paper from the operator. Or you could use Lotus 1-2-3 and SPSS as a statistic program on a terminal.

In my first job as an assistant auditor I created a card game program on a Macintosh just for fun during lunch hours. Do not ask me what

---

[1] Unlike my other books, there is no separate literature list as much information can be found on line or is common knowledge.

program I used. I also worked on an IBM machine to add the amounts of invoices. Privately I used programs on the Apple II c and various MS Dos/Windows machines.

You may have read my book 'Connecting Consumer Devices through the Ages' which describes computers and their hardware from the 1980's until the present and focusses on the way the parts of the computer and peripherals communicate. This book also deals with computers in that same period but focusses on the software, data and programs used by those computers. The hardware is interesting and a necessity but the software makes the computer function and adds value to every one of us. Looking at this previous book I will describe the software used in §3.3 'Personal computer' like the Apple computer and the Microsoft computer. I will not describe the software (or applications) used in §3.4 for the iPad, Chromebook and iPhone as these are mostly variations of programs used on the traditional computer. I will describe device drivers used in §6 which is software. In addition to the previous book I will also describe software used on mainframes with terminals. I have tried not to overlap too much in this new book so you can read it separately. When you are done reading, you can fill in the list of the software and devices you have used yourself in attachment 1, just for fun.

The chapters of this book can be shown graphically:

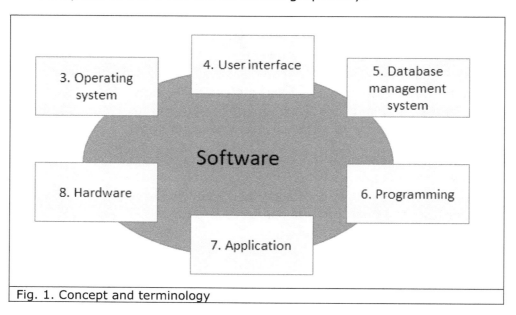

Fig. 1. Concept and terminology

2. Concept and Terminology

The terms of the title and subtitle of this book 'software' and 'computer programs' are very generic. I have used sources as https://csrc.nist.gov/glossary and https://www.techopedia.com/dictionary but I prefer to change these terms a little and describe them myself.

I describe **software** as programs and associated **data** that may be dynamically written or modified during the computers' execution. Data can be stored in a database. Software can also run on non-PC devices like a dishwasher but that is outside the scope of this book.

The **operating system** is a collection of software as integrated service routines that manages computer hardware resources and provides common services for computer programs. The applications communicate with the operating system for most user interface and file management operations.

A **program** or **applicatio**n is software that can be executed in real time. It is used for collecting, saving, processing, and presenting data by means of a computer. A program can also be used solely by another program and therefore not always needs a user interface.
Programming means writing your own application mostly in a special programming language.

The **browser** is a generic user interface to access web pages, databases or other data. An application can be easier to develop and maintain if a browser is used to interact with the user. Browsers translate web pages and websites delivered using Hypertext Transfer Protocol (HTTP) into human-readable content.

A database or **database management system** is software designed to store, retrieve, query and manage data which can have the format of records.

A **user interface** is software to interact between the user and any kind of the above mentioned kinds of software.

The relation between the various types of software is discussed further on at the subject of operating system.

3. Operating system

3.1.   Introduction

An operating system is a specific kind of software that is needed to run other software or applications on an electronic device. Before any program can start, the operating system has to run. The first thing that activates when you turn on the switch of your computer is the boot loader. Microsoft (MS) Windows has a boot loader and so do MacOS and Linux. The boot loader is stored in the Read Only Memory (ROM) and is loaded into the Random Access memory (RAM) in various stages. In the first stage or hardware initialization stage the boot loader[2] loads the system firmware, the Basic Input Output System (BIOS). The second stage boot loader loads the operating system(s) and device drivers. Examples of boot loaders are GNU Grub for Linux and BootMRG for MS Windows (Vista and higher).

Functions of the operating system are[3]:

Function	Description
Booting	Managing the startup of a device.
Loading and execution	Starting and executing a program.
Memory management	Coordinating applications and allocating memory space to installed programs.
Drive/disk management	Managing drives and disks. Keep information on all files in the File Allocation table (FAT).
User interface	The visual way users interact with the programs. This can be a command line interface or graphical user interface.
Data security	Protecting data from cyberattacks. Providing security by shielding off user accounts and passwords.
Device control	Allowing or blocking access to devices including buffering and spooling as the Central Processor Unit speed is much higher than a device speed.
Process management	Allocating memory space for storing and sharing information including scheduling (which program runs at what time and order).

---

[2] Booting - Wikipedia
[3] https://www.indeed.com/career-advice/career-development/types-of-operating-systems and https://www.geeksforgeeks.org/need-and-functions-of-operating-systems

Tab. 1. Functions of the operating system

An operating system, its functions and the interaction with the user can be shown as:

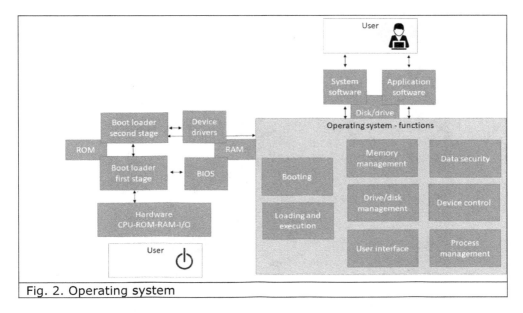

Fig. 2. Operating system

The following has not changed much over the years after you turn your computer on regardless of the type of operating system. The BIOS is powered on, the hardware will be checked, and the disk drive searches for the master boot record and finds the location of the bootable partition. When you start or shut down the computer or change the BIOS-settings, it will be registered in the Complementary metal oxide semiconductor (CMOS)-chip that is powered by a separate battery if the computer is not connected to a power outlet. The file IO.SYS initializes the disk, keyboard and screen to permit input and output of data (I/O). Next, IO.SYS calls MSDOS.SYS. MS-DOS.SYS is basically the kernel of the operating system. After initializing, MS-DOS.SYS then calls COMMAND.COM. COMMAND.COM initializes and reads the batch file AUTOEXEC.BAT to determine what environment settings are required, such as the PATH variable. The PATH tells the system where to look for valid programs. If a program is not located within the path, you will have to type in the drive letter, path and filename information in order to launch the program.

Your MS-Dos computer would stop at the command line with the cursor at the prompt like C:/>. Then it was up to you to type the command to go to the directory where the application was installed if not defined by the PATH and type a command as the name of an EXE-file. The computer would start with a screen like this:

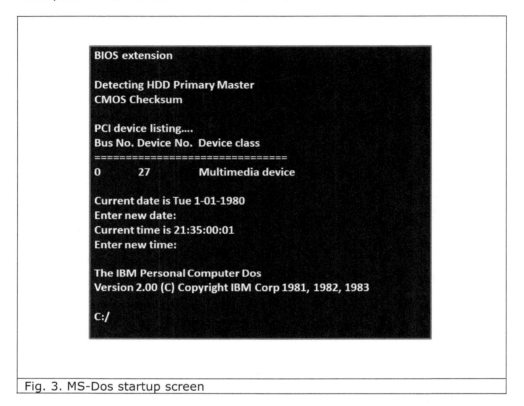

Fig. 3. MS-Dos startup screen

3.2.   Types of operating systems

Before I started to use MS Windows I had experience with MS Dos as well as with the Apple's Macintosh Operating system (Mac OS). Actually nobody talked about Mac OS as you could not give commands in the OS because the Mac OS was shielded off and users could only use programs on the Mac to work with the computer. Another thing that was always remarkable to me was that the Mac did not have a way to access a document from an explorer like MS Dos and MS Windows and you could only access it from a program. The program on the Mac OS was connected to certain types of documents that you could change yourself in MS Windows and MS Dos by the file type of the document. Also a difference was that you could open a text with more than one program like Write or Word on the Mac and in MS Dos it was related to one program only. There are many differences in the way the user interacts with the operating system in that way.

What operating system you prefer is very personal and mostly based on your experience. As I started with MS Dos and MS Windows it is my number 1 choice to work with on documents. I do like the iOS and Android for browsing and the various apps that they offer as you can use your finger to navigate between windows. The systems have their different way for updates which can be a little annoying but once your IPad or IPhone is not supported by the latest version of iOS it soon loses functionality for new apps and security. That might be the same for Android but I haven't noticed that yet. On the other hand if MS Windows 11 states that your hardware is unsupported there are ways to get around it but by that time is makes more sense to get a new lap/desktop. The Window apps that appeared starting at MS Windows 7 have never gotten my liking. I prefer the software like MS word compared to a word app with less functionality. Generally it is easier to change system setting on MS Windows than on Android or iOS.

As far as I remember MS used the idea of the Mac in showing multiple windows on your screen for multiple programs. That was quite a change from MS Dos where you had to type in a command on the prompt line.

There are some noticeable differences between the two platforms as explained in https://www.pcmag.com/news/macos-vs-windows-which-os-really-is-the-best

aspect	MacOS	MS Windows	my experience
installation	with or without an Apple account	with or without an Windows account	I prefer no account as I do not want to share my information with these companies though synchronizing of settings between devices is harder
start apps, access documents	pin apps to the dock	with the start button	
hardware	limited	wide	a variety of models and

	choice and pricey	selection	brands for various prices
apps included	comparable		I prefer programs instead of apps as they have more functionality and you do not have to update them as frequently
navigation	Dock	Taskbar	I find the taskbar more restful when you use the mouse over.
file management	Finder	File explorer	With the right click in Windows you can decide with which program to open the kind of file.
stability	Apple controls the hardware ecosystem	third-party drivers are a major cause of instability	It's very important to use the updates and a virus/malware scanner

Tab. 2. MacOs versus MS Windows

Some of the operating systems can be compared as follows:

type	MS Dos	MS Windows	iOS	macOS (previous OSX)	Google Android	Linux i.e. Ubuntu or Redhat
Price	Free	Preloaded	Preloaded	Preloaded	Preloaded	Free
devices	IBM compatible	Desktop and laptop	Iphone and ipad	Apple and Macintosh	Smart phone and tablet with Google OS on a Chromebook	Desktop and laptop
Graphical user interface	Non, command line	yes	yes	yes	yes	yes
% used[4]	none	31	16	6	41	1
Default browser	none	Edge (like Chrome)	Safari	Safari	Chrome	Firefox

Tab. 3. Compare operating systems

---

[4] Operating System Market Share Worldwide | Statcounter Global Stats april 2022

3.3.   *History of Microsoft Dos and Windows*

MS Dos relied much on batch files that you could write yourself. I did so for a simple menu that would turn up as you started the program and a favorite command line was *'bright white on blue'* for the font color of the menu and the background color of the screen. It was also needed to change two files CONFIG.SYS and AUTOEXIG.BAT for settings with a simple editor (notepad). CONFIG.SYS is a text file for setup and configuration of devices and applications.

Common commands in these files were:

```
@ECHO OFF                                 NUMLOCK=OFF
PROMPT $p$g                               BREAK=ON
PATH C:\WINDOWS;C:\WINDOWS\COMMAND        DOS=HIGH,UMB,NOAUTO
SET DIRCMD=/P /A                          FILES=10
SET TEMP=C:\WINDOWS\TEMP                  BUFFER=10
```

- Hides the text in batch programs when the batch file is executed.
- Set the DOS prompt to show the current directory followed by the character >.
- Indicates in which directories and in which order programs shall be searched for.
- Sets the DOS DIR command for pausing, when the screen becomes full, and to display all files .
- States in which directory temporary files can be placed by the applications.

- Switches off Num Lock on the keyboard.
- Extends Control to work for reading and writing disks.
- HIGH loads DOS buffers in HMA . UMB allows the use of Upper Memory Blocks for resident drivers and programs.
- Specifies the number of files that can be opened at once.
- Specifies the number of disk buffers to allocate.

Tab. 4. CONFIG.SYS and AUTOEXEC.BAT

The CONFIG.SYS was later replaced by the Windows registry as a hierarchical database. You can still edit it but it is a little more tricky.

The most significant versions of MS Windows were[5]:

version	year	bits	RAM	my experience
1.0	1985-2001	16	256 Kb	it used the mouse and multitasking with overlapping 'tiled' windows
3.1	1992-2001	16	1 Mb	this is the earliest version I remember and I am not quite sure how it interacted with MS Dos as later versions of MS Windows did not need MS Dos any more.
95	1995-	16/32	4 Mb	integration of Dos and Windows with long file names
ME	2000-2011	16/32	32 Mb	
7	2009-2020	32/64	I Gb (32b) 2 Gb (64b)	this was the version where it would start with a tablet screen of tiles and unless you know how to do it you could not easily get back to the traditional menu structure and start your programs. This was the period when touch screens became popular and instead of using the mouse to start a program you might want to do this by touching the tile with your fingers. I believe it was too early for the big public and people did not like it.
10	2015-2025	32/64	I Gb (32b) 2 Gb (64b)	apps versus programs. These aps can also run on other devices besides a computer. They do not always offer the full functionality though. It also meant the end of Internet Explorer which has been replaced with Edge.

Tab. 5. Versions of MS Windows

Here is an overview of screenshots of the most significant versions:

---

[5] Pages like https://en.wikipedia.org/wiki/Windows_1.0x

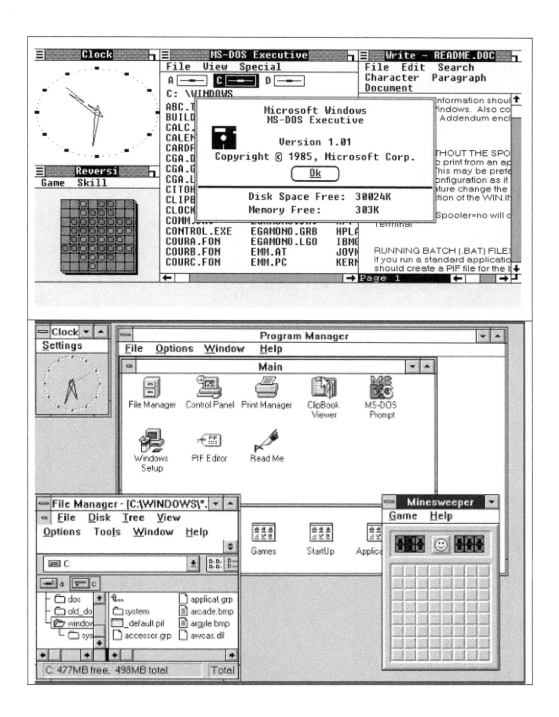

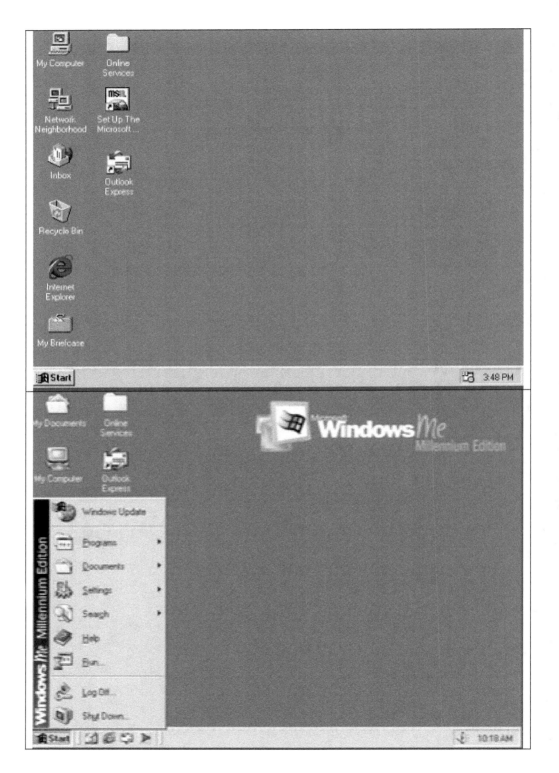

Fig. 4. MS Windows 1.0, 3.1, 95, ME, 7 and 10

4 User interface

4.1. Textual user or command line interface

There are various ways the user can interact with the computer and send a command or instruction to make the computer process data. A click on an input device creates a command with any key or combination of keys on the keyboard or the mouse like described in my book 'Connecting'.[6] These can be the alphanumeric keys as well as the special keys like Esc, F1-F12, Fn, ctrl, alt, delete and insert that create a virtual-key code used by the system.[7] The F1-F12 keys were very usefully before MS Windows and the mouse were available as they were shortcuts for example for WordPerfect when pulldown menus were not yet available to select with the pointer or mouse. Combination of the F-key with the Ctrl, Shift or Alt key would offer even more possibilities. It was quite common to stick a template on your keyboard to remind you what the command was for each F-key like in WordPerfect 5.1[8]:

key	F1	F2	F3	F4
normal	cancel	search	help	indent
shift	setup	search	switch	indent
alt	thesaurus	replace	reveal codes	block
ctrl	shell	shell	screen	move
key	F5	F6	F7	F8
normal	list	bold	exit	underline
shift	date/outline	center	print	format
alt	mark text	flush right	column/table	style
ctrl	text in/out	tab align	footnote	font
key	F9	F10	F11	F12
normal	end field	save		
shift	merge codes	retrieve	reveal codes	block
alt	graphics	macro		

[6] See also the chapter on hardware in this book.
[7] See i.e. https://learn.microsoft.com/en-us/windows/win32/inputdev/virtual-key-codes
[8] https://geeksontour.com/2022/09/whatever-happened-to-word-processing/

ctrl	merge/sort	macro define		

Tab. 6. F-keys WordPerfect

The function of these combinations has changed. MS Word 2016 uses the following[9]:

key	F1	F2	F3	F4
normal	help	move text or object	auto text entry	repeat
shift	formatting pane	copy selected text	switch case of selected text	repeat last find
alt	jump next field		create auto text	quit program
ctrl	Expand or collapse the ribbon.	print window	cut selected text	close document
key	F5	F6	F7	F8
normal	find and replace	next pane or frame	spelling and grammar check	selection mode
shift	jump previous edit	previous pane or frame	thesaurus	reduce selection
alt	Restore the program window size.	Move from an open dialog box back to the document	next spelling or grammar error	Run a macro.
ctrl		next open document		insert field
key	F9	F10	F11	F12
normal	update field	key tips	jump next field	save as window
shift	reveal field code	context menu	jump previous field	save as document
alt	toggle display field code	Display the Selection task pane.	Display Microsoft Visual Basic code.	

19

ctrl	insert empty field	maximize window	lock field	open window

Tab. 7. F-keys MS Word

You might notice that hardly any of the combination of the keys has the same function nowadays. F5 is very convenient to refresh the screen of your browser.

4.2.   Graphical user interface

A lot changed when it became possible to click on a command from a menu mostly due to a technical change in the resolution of the screen. Here the development of software and hardware interact when the resolution changed from like 80 columns and 24 lines of text to 560 x 192 up to 1.600 x 900 pixels what is quiet normal nowadays. Icons can be shown, backgrounds can be detailed, movies can be shown and even pictures can be used.

4.3.   Language of the interface

Most people like to interact with their computer in their native language like Dutch in my case. But most operating languages and applications are written in English to be able to use it worldwide. Some languages are only used by a small population so it would not be worthwhile to offer different languages. Let's assume all the text for the user interface has been made available in Dutch as well as English. The words may have become larger or more in Dutch and if the font is not scalable, how can you make sure it will fit right on the screen? I can imagine an option with two versions of the OS where you would use the Dutch words in a separate version of the source code and have it compiled once or have a table of the English and Dutch commands and have it compiled as soon as the user switches the language. These problems seem to have overcome during the years and I have researched if and in what languages Dos and MS Windows have been made available. As far as I remember MS Dos always came in the Netherlands in the English version and MS Windows in the Dutch version. As both operating systems were mostly pre-installed on the computer, you would have to reinstall the OS extra in another language if you wanted to and pay for it extra. Later on their were more language packs offered like Dutch,

English, French and German on one computer so when you started the computer you could (one time) set your preferred language. The same with MS Office. It did not automatically mean that you would be able to check your spelling and grammar in that language as well so it was a lot of hassle in the early days. Nowadays you can just choose your language and you can change it later again if you wish.

I do remember we used the English version of FOCUS as system managers and the end users would use the Dutch version they preferred as MS Windows was also in installed in Dutch. It could take a while though between solving issues in the English version and translating it by the manufacturer in the Dutch version. A problem in the software was fixed that way but not yet available for the end user.

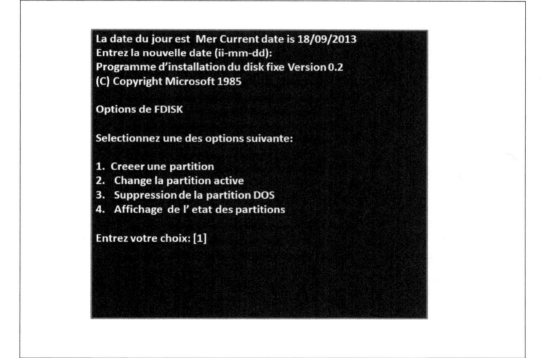

La date du jour est Mer Current date is 18/09/2013
Entrez la nouvelle date (ii-mm-dd):
Programme d'installation du disk fixe Version 0.2
(C) Copyright Microsoft 1985

Options de FDISK

Selectionnez une des options suivante:

1. Creeer une partition
2. Change la partition active
3. Suppression de la partition DOS
4. Affichage de l' etat des partitions

Entrez votre choix: [1]

Fig. 5. MS-Dos in French

You might wonder in what languages MS DOS and MS Windows came and still are available? That is the user interface language and not necessarily the language under the hood in the operating system itself in which the OS is written. MS Dos came in 84 (!) languages though you might only know the English version and your national language version[10].

That is not the same as the languages you can type with the keyboard as there are many more of those.

4.4.   (web) Browser

The browser is the interface to browse through webpages. Some of the most popular browsers were:

	Netscape	Internet Explorer	Chrome	Edge	Firefox (follow up on Netscape)
year from - until	1994-2008	1995-2014	2008-today	2015-today	2002-today
operating system	MS Windows, macos, os/2, linux	MS Windows, macos, unix	MS Windows, macos, ios, linux, android	MS Windows, macos, ios, linux, android	MS Windows, macos, ios, linux, android

Tab. 8. Browsers

Internet Explorer was one of the first browsers but there were not many options to change its behavior. Google Chrome made it possible to use extensions like a block for commercials and the option to translate a page or document. You could also change some experimental settings so it became my favorite. Internet explorer was succeeded by Edge which is not much more than Google Chrome for MS Windows. Firefox is another nice browser with many add-ons if you want to get away from Microsoft.

---

[10] https://fo.wikipedia.org/wiki/Serstakt:MobileLanguages/MS-DOS

5 Data and data base management system

Data has been mentioned before in relation to programming as occurrences of variables that decide the flow of the program and interact with the user and other programs. Like i.e. the color of your screen or font. Other uses of data are the content of free format files like a word document or structured format files a like a data base. These files can have a certain size and a length of the filename as will be explained. A data base management system consists of the actual database and the software to use and manage the database.

Size of file

The maximum size of a file and the amount of content it can store is dependent upon factors like the file system. A modern File Allocation Table (FAT) 32 system allows up to 4 Gb of data in one file.

Length of filenames

In the past you could only use up to eight characters for the filename and three characters for the file extension i.e. AUTOEXEC.BAT. It would also situationally matter if you used upper or lower case characters. Since the arrival of MS Windows 95 the file name can be up to 260 positions. MS Windows 11 even allows 32,767 characters for a filename which can be set in the registry with 'long path enabled'. The length of the file name is related to the File allocation Table (FAT).

The file extension was always used to connect a program to a specific file type like link .DOC for a word document to a word processor. The user could change this manually according to his or her preference.

On the DEC VAX a file could be saved with a name, extension and version i.e. STORY.TXT.1. That made it easier to keep different versions of a document instead of renaming the file name with a number.

Queries on the database

I worked on databases for the central government between 1988 and 1998 so I guess I can write freely about it by now. I was a data administrator and data base administrator in those days. In my studies I learned about logical data models with entities, attributes and relations.

That helped me a lot to create databases and use queries on the financial system. Even in my dissertation many years later I used a logical model to illustrate how an identity is made up from identifiers.

The financial system
I used queries most of all to create financial reports and one time to migrate the DB2-database from an old to a new format. The DB2-database ran on a mainframe and was used for the financial system with the modules of internal budget, external budget and debtors/creditors. The local Rdb-database was used for data entry of invoices, receivables and commitments. The data from the local database would be uploaded to the central database at the end of the day and both databases would be synchronized. The reason for a central/local solution was as the communication lines had a limited capacity and was expensive to use at a higher capacity. Special land lines were hired to communicate between specific buildings (our department versus the data center).

IBM/DB2
Query Management Facility-in (QMF) was the tool I used for the IBM DB2-database. The F1-F12 keys as mentioned elsewhere were very useful to start commands. It is a database-independent language that allows you to query data and to perform CRUD (Create, Update, and Delete) operations. You could also grant and revoke access to a table. A simple query in QMF would be 'select * from table where x = y'. You would then get a table of results but not in a way that an end user had any benefit from it. After that you would create a report by adding a form to the result which would make subtotals, headers, footers, etc. To create a report you would say 'run query (form=x)' and you had a report. You could then print it. As our machine capacity was limited and in order not to interfere with the end user using the menu of the financial system, I would run these in the background at night in the batch. If it was a complicated query that would take too long to run, I did it in subqueries. like run query 1 save the result as a table 1, run query 2, etc. than the final query would be to select records from table 1, 2, etc. and save the procedures so the service desk could run them every month for the end user to help them.

One time the financial system was totally updated with a new database structure, I queried the old tables to save data. Then I created a new database with SQL in the required format and fill it step by step in a certain order to fill the news fields and records. I had created reports before to check the number and values of the records before and after. This was quite a challenge and I do not think this could happen nowadays with one person in charge of the whole process of renewing the database! I convinced my boss that I could do it for free instead of paying thousands of guilders to consultants.

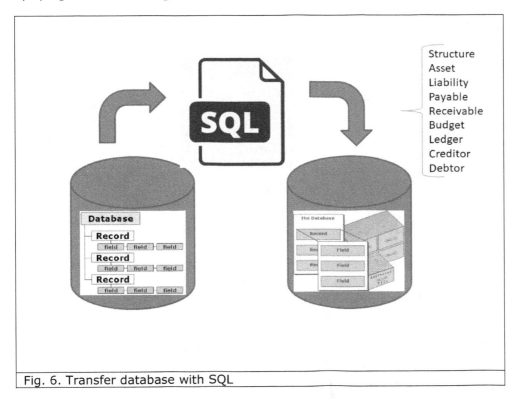

Structure
Asset
Liability
Payable
Receivable
Budget
Ledger
Creditor
Debtor

Fig. 6. Transfer database with SQL

I was quite proud of myself and think this is still the highlight of my career as a civil servant!

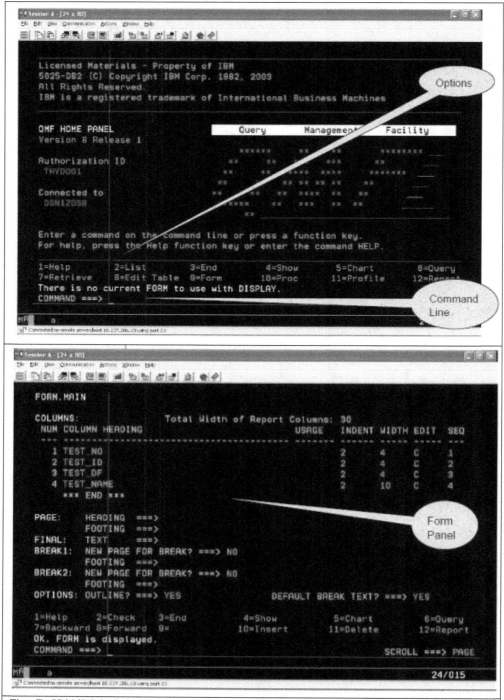

Fig. 7. IBM/DB2 © https://www.ibmmainframer.com/db2-tutorial/db2-qmf/

VAX Rdb

I also ran queries on another local Rdb database for which I made a daily export of the updates from the central database for the relevant data. For the Digital VAX Rdb-database there were no facilities but to write your own program. I used it to make an application with Rally Rdb and Datatrieve so I could give the user the report online and print what they needed instead of the formal reports going through the development procedure and they did not get what they needed. I also make control programs to synchronize the local database with the central database by using hash totals.

And we used FOCUS from Information Builders so end users could make their own queries and reports. It was a little tricky as you always needed some insight in the datamodel before you could make a valid report.

6. Programming

Programming starts from scratch by designing a program and writing in a programming language to create your own, private software. The level or generation of programming varies from machine language all the way up to natural language. I have grouped the ones I know and have used as follows:

Generation	Description
1. Machine or low	I used machine language on the Apple II c where you would type a bunch of 0's and 1's hoping that I would not make a typo but none of these programs worked as there was no way to check errors. This language would differ dependent on the hardware you would use. It can be executed right away.
2. Assembly or very low	I have not used this level and I seems that these languages were or are only used for hard drives etc. It needed an assembler to convert instructions to machine language.
3. High level or third generation	Basic, Fortran, Pascale, C, Cobol and JavaScript. It needed a compiler of interpreter to convert instructions to machine language.
4. Very high level or fourth generation (4GL)	For example SQL
5. Natural	This did not exist yet in the days I used to program.

Tab. 9. Programming language generation

There is always a design issue as I would say and that means how you interact data with programs. I.e. you want to write a program that shows the name of the day depending on the number of the day. You could do that like:

Print 'Monday' if daynumber =1
Print 'Tuesday' if daynumber =2
Etc.

This first method is called hard coding. Another option is to take the value of the variables out of the program and store this in a text file

The textfile like NAMEDAY.TXT would consist of '1 Monday, 2 Tuesday'.

The program would then be

Read NAMEDAY.TXT daynumber dayname
Print Nameday (number of the day).

It would then be possible to later change the content of NAMEDAT.TXT without changing the program. This way data or variables can be changed independent of the program and the source code of the program stays the same where you do not have to compile the program again. This prevents errors in reprogramming and makes it possible for the end user to change the values of variables. And as the source code might not be there it is easier to check for values of variables.

Basic was a better program to use and you would find programs in special magazines to retype and save on your computer. Fortran, Pascal and Cobol were used at the university still on punch cards. Dbase was a good way to program in a structure. I remember making a program for a sauna which was a lot of fun to do so. Developing a website was done with HTML for a simple site and if you wanted to make it fancier you could interact with JavaScript. I also used it to write a program to open up documents on a cd-rom with a nice user interface. We handed them out in large quantities through the auditing department.

I remember using Datatrieve (as well as Rally/Rdb) on the Vax with the databases I created locally in order to make reports for end users. The 566 p (!) manual is still available on internet for those who want to take a look at it[11].

The way programming works is very well explained in https://homepage.cs.uri.edu/faculty/wolfe/book/programming/chapsix.html by Victor Fay-Wolfe Fall2005 of the University of Rhode Island so it would not have any additional value to copy the text in this book.

---

[11] https://sector7.com/s7/Reference/VMS_Manuals/DATATRIEVE_Reference_Manual.pdf

7. Application software

7.1.   *Programs versus apps*

Software like MS Word is a ready to use 'commercial of the shelf' program with a user interface and many functions that can be used by interacting of a human with the computer.

An 'App' or 'application' is a program that cannot work by itself but only in connection of other programs that are already available on your computer. The 'app' can be relatively simple and does not take up much computer storage space by itself as much common functionality is used from these other programs. The most well-known apps are the ones that are installed on your smart phone from stores like Apple Store for the iOS devices as the iPad and iPhone, Google Play for Android devices and Microsoft store for MS Windows devices. On some platforms like MS Windows 7 upwards you can choose between an app and a program.

7.2.   *All-in-1*

All-in-1 was the tool I used at work on a terminal mainly for word-processing. I don't think the electronic messaging or mail worked at least not outside our own office. Worldwide mail accounts with a @ became only available much later.

WPS Plus was used as a Word Processing System.

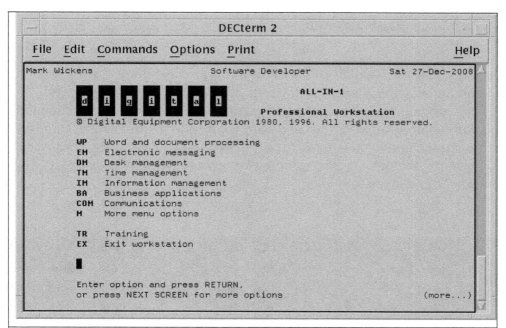

Fig. 8. All-in-1 © https://en.wikipedia.org/wiki/ALL-IN-1

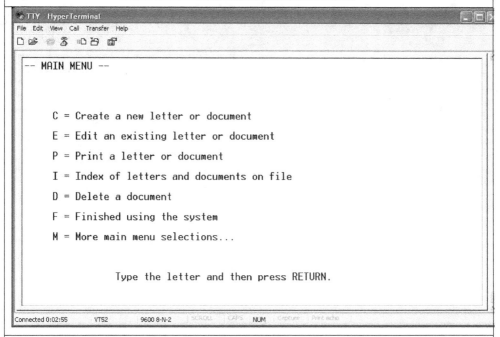

Fig. 9. WPS © https://raymii.org/s/articles/Running_WPS-8_(Word_Processing_System)_on_the_DEC(mate)_PDP-8i_and_SIMH.html

7.3.   *Appleworks*

On the Apple II c, Appleworks was an integrated program for word processing, database and spreadsheet starting in 1984. Integration meant that you could use the same commands for the same functions in the various programs. It was also easy to change a spreadsheet later on into a database and vice versa. Try to do this nowadays with Word and you lose the format. It was a good way to keep track of your music records or expenses at home.

Fig. 10. Appleworks © https://www.apple2history.org/history/ah19/

7.4. Lotus 1-2-3

```
A:A1: 'ENP                                                      MENU
Worksheet  Range  Copy  Move  File  Print  Graph  Data  System  Quit
Global  Insert  Delete  Column  Erase  Titles  Window  Status  Page  Hide
A        A          B          C          D       E         F         G
1   ENP         EMP_NAME     DEPTNO    JOB        YEARS    SALARY    BONUS
2          1777 Azil\*ad      4000 Sales      2     40000    10000
3         81964 Brown        6000 Sales      3     45000    10000
4         48370 Burns        6000 Mgr        4     75000    25000
5         58706 Caeser       7000 Mgr        3     65000    25000
6         40602 Curly        3000 Mgr        5     65000    20000
7         34701 Dabarrett    7000 Sales      2     45000    10000
8         84904 Daniels      1000 President  8    150000   100000
9         59937 Dempsey      3000 Sales      3     40000    10000
10        51515 Donovan      3000 Sales      2     30000     5000
11        48338 Fields       4000 Mgr        5     70000    25000
12        91574 Fiklore      1000 Admin      8     35000      ---
13        64506 Fine         5000 Mgr        3     75000    25000
14        13729 Green        1000 Mgr        5     90000    25000
15        55957 Hermann      4000 Sales      4     50000    10000
16        31619 Hodgedon     5000 Sales      2     40000    10000
17         1773 Howard       2000 Mgr        3     80000    25000
18         2165 Hugh         1000 Admin      5     30000      ---
19        23907 Johnson      1000 VP         1    100000    50000
20         7166 Laflare      2000 Sales      2     35000     5000
DATA.WK3
```

Fig. 11. Lotus 1-2-3 © https://nl.wikipedia.org/wiki/Lotus_1-2-3

It was possible to run the complete administration of a company in Lotus even though that was a little tricky as you can easily delete a row in a tab and your spreadsheet might be corrupt. I don't recall that Lotus allowed more than one sheet in a file like a workbook with multiple worksheets. The advantage of the last one was that you could use one sheet for the overview and make every separate sheet a lot simpler and easier to adjust.

33

7.5.   *WordPerfect*

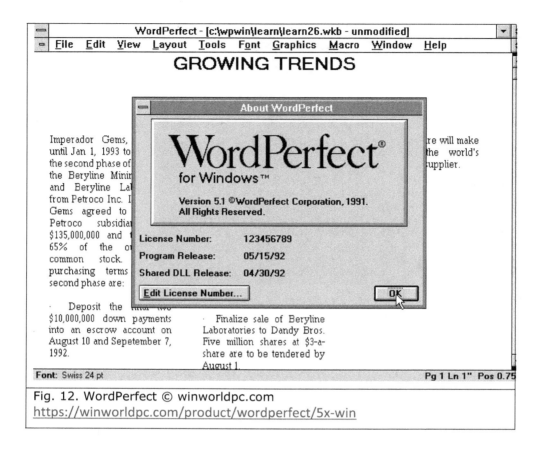

Fig. 12. WordPerfect © winworldpc.com
https://winworldpc.com/product/wordperfect/5x-win

7.6.   *Mail*

Mail was and is one of the most used programs to interact and send messages since the internet started. Before it was only possible to fax which was sometimes supported by a 'mail' program as well. Besides the protocols for mail over the internet like SMTP. POP3 and IMAP there was X.400 since 1984 for dedicated networks between companies. The unique address of a X.400 mailbox is a little more complicated than an email address and can consist of a combination of surname, given name, organization, domain and country. I remember using them for a short period of time. Internet mail addresses are simpler like (the non existing) Clemens.Willemsen@internet.com.

Simple Mail Transfer Protocol (SMTP) is the most used protocol to send mail from one mail address to another mail address. SMTP requires that the receiver is always connected to the internet which is in fact the mailbox at your provider. Receiving the mail when you connect to the internet is done by Post Office Protocol (POP3) or Internet Message Access Protocol (IMAP). POP3 downloads the messages from the server, saves them on your computer and deletes them by standard from the server. IMAP has this same disconnected mode but also a connected mode where the messages are kept at the server. SMTP only supports ASCII-text and it uses Multipurpose Internet Mail Extensions (MIME) to add content like photo, video, etc.

This way storage of data moved in time from local to central also works for mail. You used to get an account from your internet provider to receive and store your mail online. You could then download it automatically to the one computer and access it with i.e. Outlook Express. The mail address from the provider was not so convenient as it is still not for all providers accessible with a app on your portable device. Mail from your provider also had a disadvantage if you would change from provider then you could not continue to use your mail or you had to pay extra for it. I had many different mail addresses in the past which was not such a big issue until the times came that websites started to oblige you to log in with a username or mail address and password. That's why many people used an extra and more permanent mail address like from Gmail or Yahoo. They are free but how free and safe are they really? These vendors try to lure you to use paid options and other programs. They might also use your private data for other purposes so that is the downfall.

The various mail programs do not use the same format to store their data so it can be an issue if you want to change our mail program and/or move your mail to another computer. I remember that when Outlook Express (OE) as a included part of MS Windows was replaced with MS Outlook as part of MS Office. OE uses a .dbx file extension and Outlook a .pst format. There are tools that can help you to convert your mail to another format. OE only had mail and newsgroups which is sufficient for personal use. Outlook had mail, calendar and contacts so better to be used in a business environment.

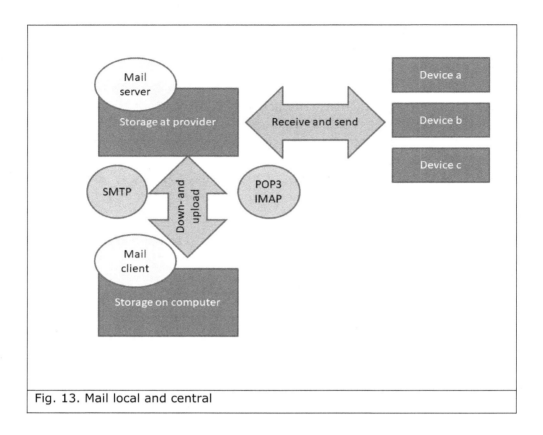

Fig. 13. Mail local and central

A reason for downloading mail was also that in the beginning you had to pay per minute of per byte for the internet connection so you wanted to view your mail offline when possible. Programs for mail were and are: MS Outlook, Gmail, Opera, MS Windows mail, Yahoo and Thunderbird.

There is a distinction between the mail program and the account you can use to access the mail. For a long time it was i.e. possible to use a Gmail account and Outlook as the program to download and access your mail.

7.7.   *Microsoft Office*

MS Office consists of MS Word, MS Excel. MS PowerPoint, MS Outlook, MS Access and MS Publisher

Microsoft presents the various applications as a whole though these started in fact as independent programs and therefore you might notice differences in the way commands work. The origin of the programs is as follows:

application	original name	original platform	first version	first version for MS Windows
word	multi-tool word	Unix	1983	1989
excel	multiplan	MS DOS	1985	1987
powerpoint	presenter	MacOS	1987	1989
outlook	exchange client	MS DOS	1992	1997
access	cirrus	ms windows	1992	1992

7.8.   Open office – Libre Office

MS Office has to be paid for by a license. Open Office is free and has almost the same functionality. I remember it looked a little less smooth than MS Office and some actions like mail merge were limited but if you were looking for a cheap alternative then Open Office was a program to consider. Later it turned into Libre Office.

Open Office can be compared with MS Office:

- Writer – Word

- Calc – Excel

- Base – Access

- Draw – MS Publisher

- Impress –Powerpoint

- Math – n.a.

7.9.   Price of software

The price of software or how vendors make you pay for using their software has changed significantly during the years. Mostly if you would buy a (desk top) computer, the operating system was preinstalled and

37

also available on a bunch of diskettes as a backup and to reinstall. Later MS Windows might not always come with the hardware or as an extra option that you had to pay for. Packages like Microsoft Office has to be paid for separately. Upgrades of operating systems and application software would come as a set of diskettes or later on CD-ROM. This would continue until the internet connections where fast enough to download the newer software to your computer. I must say, the need for (security) update was less than now as you are connected to the internet and have more chance of malware that can infect your computer. I state that the safest computer is the one that is not connected to the internet! The need for an update of functionality was less than compared to now it seems.

So you would pay one time when you purchased the software and that would last a long time until there was a new release of the program. The support would also end after that period. There would be a difference for businesses with many users as you would pay a fee for every user of the software. You might also be limited to install the program on one or more devices.

Later on besides paid for software there would be freeware that you could download and use without payment or license. There might be a catch in this like limited functionality, limited time to use, limited support and of course you could not always tell if it was safe to use. Another option was and is open software that does not cost anything, is maintained by a community and has a forum for questions. For example Open Office that I describe earlier or Thunderbird.

Besides or instead of a onetime payment companies like Microsoft use a monthly payment of their software like office 365. You can calculate what you pay over the years that you use it but then everything is included. For apps that you buy in the Google Play store or Apple store you have the options too of a limited app of a full app with payment.

	freeware	*open source*	*paid one time*	*paid periodically*
price	none	none	large amount	small amount but continuousl y
updates	free	free	during the life cycle	free

support	limited	community	extensively during the life cycle	extensively
functionality	can be limited or with adds	sometimes less than for paid software	full	full

Tab. 10. Price of software

8. Software versus hardware

8.1.   Introduction

Though this book is about software, there is a relation with hardware in some aspects as mentioned for example in the chapter on operating systems. Some of those aspects I will address but i will not be complete about the relation.

Aspects are:

2. Running software on one of more hardware platforms
3. Cloud (service) computing models
4. Firmware and embedded software
5. Number of bits of software versus hardware
6. Device drivers
7. Quantum computing

8.2.   Software on various hardware platforms

You might wonder if it is possible to run the various types of software on various brands of computers. Do you have to use IOS on an IPad and MS Windows on a desktop or are there alternatives and what makes software work on different platforms or not?

A simple question would be: what operating system (OS) can run on what device or hardware platform? Or can you install and use multiple operating systems on one hardware platform? A hardware platform consists of het central processor unit (CPU), Read Only Memory (ROM), Random Access Memory (RAM), etc. The answer is not easy to find on the internet. The question would be more precisely: what are the hardware requirements for a specific type of operating system? Instead of 'hardware platform' the term 'computer architecture' is also used.

The various generations of a OS require minimum capabilities of the hardware (hardware compatibility list) like: the brand and type of CPU with a certain clock frequency in GHz and X-bit support, the (primary) amount of RAM in Megabytes (Mb), the amount of (secondary) storage space in Mb, the graphics processing unit (GPU), a (optical) disk drive, etc. If the requirements are not met then you can sometimes upgrade a certain hardware component or you need a totally new mother board on which these components are mounted.

Some particular OS's are architecture independent but most need to be 're-compiled' to run on a new architecture[12].

Multiple different OS's or different versions of one OS can be installed on the same computer in different partitions of the hard disk (or installed on different drives) but only one can be used at the same time and the user must make a choice each time with software called the 'boot loader'[13]. Another more complicated way to use more OS's is the use of a virtual machine but then extra hardware might be required. So you can have MS Windows as well as Linux on one computer or MS Windows 7 and MS Windows 8 on that same computer.

8.3.   *Cloud (service) computing*

Cloud (service) computing is about the location of hardware and software components. It is also known as cloud infrastructure or cloud architecture. Traditionally all the components were at your own location, 'on premises', like a data center. The three distinctive cloud service models expand from infrastructure as a service (IaaS) by platform as a service (PaaS) to software as a service (Saas) as can be seen in the figure. In spite of its name PaaS hosts the operating system and SaaS the application and data(base). An example of IaaS is Amazon web services. An example of PaaS is Microsoft Azure. Examples of SaaS are Microsoft Office 365, Gmail and Dropbox. As this book is about software I will focus on the location of the OS and the applications and not go on with cloud computing. https://k21academy.com/amazon-web-services/aws-solutions-architect/cloud-service-models/

---

[12] Software and Hardware Requirements - Tutorial (vskills.in)
[13] Article - Can I run more than one Ope... (mines.edu)

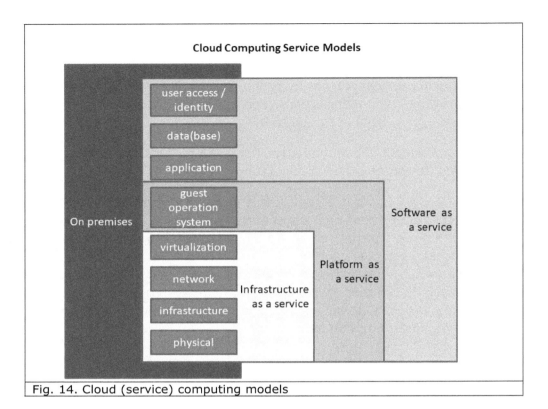

Fig. 14. Cloud (service) computing models

Application virtualization is a technique that allows application software to run on a different location and platform than the operating system. All disk operations are redirected to a virtualization location. Like for example Citrix for the MS Windows platform. It might not always work depending on a device driver, addressing the memory or licensing. It can be regarded as a client-server connection.[14]

Where to store your data

In the past you would have one computer and all the data was store on disks or on the hard drive with a backup on a another location if you remembered to make a backup frequently. Since we want to access our date anytime, anyplace, anywhere there are more options to do so. Many vendors offer an on line data drive like software manufacturers as Apple, Google, Microsoft, etc. That is storage in the cloud and can be accessed from any device. It is convenient though less secure.

---

[14] https://en.wikipedia.org/wiki/Application_virtualization

	Apple	Google	Microsoft	Dropbox	Mega (Facebook)
tool	iCloud	Drive (or One)	OneDrive	Dropbox	Cloud
capacity	5 Gb	15 Gb	5 Gb	2 Gb	20 Gb
price	free	free	free	free	free
capacity	50Gb	100 Gb	100 Gb	2 Tb	400 Gb
price	€1/month	€2/month	€2/month	€10/month	€5/month

Tab. 11. Online data drives

8.4. *Firmware and embedded software*

The chapter on operating systems has already mentioned the BIOS as firmware which is a special kind of embedded software. Embedded software is a piece of software that is embedded in hardware, written specifically for the particular hardware that it runs on. Embedded software can be very simple, such as that is used for controlling lighting in homes or complex in aircraft avionics systems. It is usually tied to a specific device, serving as the OS itself, with restrictions tied to that device's specifications. Firmware is a type of embedded software that is stored directly in a piece of hardware to make the hardware work as intended. Firmware is programmed by the manufacturer and is installed on a digital device right in the factory. It is written in non-volatile memory (such as ROM or EPROM), which cannot easily be modified — hence the name "firm" — and is used primarily for running or booting up the device. Firmware can only work with a basic or low level, binary language known as machine language. Manufacturers later on switched to using Erasable Programmable Read-Only Memory (EPROM) chips, which allowed for firmware updates[15].

In my book 'Connecting Consumer Devices through the Ages', chapter 2 I have written about memory in a physical way as a component. The different kinds of embedded software differ as the type of memory differs so I will discuss this subject more in detail.

ROM is read-only, it cannot be changed; it is permanent and non-volatile, meaning it also holds its memory even when power is removed. By contrast, random access memory (RAM) is volatile; it is lost when

---

[15] https://www.techopedia.com/dictionary

power is removed. The following table shows the differences between the two types of memory:

Subject	RAM	ROM
Data retention	RAM is a volatile memory which could store the data as long as the power is supplied.	ROM is a non-volatile memory which could retain the data even when power is turned off.
Working type	Data stored in RAM can be retrieved and altered.	Data stored in ROM can only be read.
Use	Used to store the data that has to be currently processed by CPU temporarily.	It stores the instructions required during bootstrap of the computer.
Speed	It is a high-speed memory.	It is much slower than the RAM.
CPU Interaction	The CPU can access the data stored on it.	The CPU can not access the data stored on it unless the data is stored in RAM.
Size and Capacity	Large size with higher capacity, with respect to ROM	Small size with less capacity, with respect to RAM
Used as/in	CPU Cache, Primary memory.	Firmware, Micro-controllers
Accessibility	The data stored is easily accessible	The data stored is not as easily accessible as in RAM
Cost	Costlier	cheaper than RAM.
Storage	A RAM chip can store only a few gigabytes (GB) of data.	A ROM chip can store multiple megabytes (MB) of data.

Tab. 12. RAM versus ROM © https://www.geeksforgeeks.org/difference-between-ram-and-rom

Most sources of information only show the logical and capacity aspects of the kinds of memory and only a few tell more about the difference in design. Two so called chip select input controls (CS) will enable the chip only when the microprocessor enables it. CS1 must have the value 1 and CS2 the value 0 in order to write or read. The 8-bit bidirectional data bus allows the transfer of data either from memory to the CPU during a read operation or from the CPU to memory during a write operation. A 128 * 8 RAM chip in this example has a memory capacity of 128 words of eight bits (one byte) per word. The ROM chip can only be read.[16]

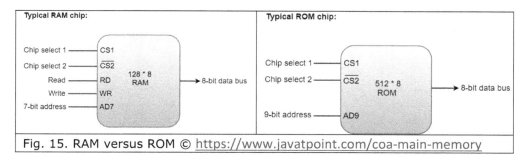

Fig. 15. RAM versus ROM © https://www.javatpoint.com/coa-main-memory

8.5. Device drivers

In my book 'Connecting Consumer Devices through the Ages', chapter 6, I have mentioned device drivers as communication software between a high level program or application and the hardware controller. The driver is mostly written in a programming language like C and distributed by the company that supplies the device. In order to install or update a driver, Microsoft Windows uses software named a 'device manager' and there are programs like this for other operating systems like Android and Linux as well.

8.6. Number of bits

The number of bits of the operating system is related to the number of bits of the processor of the computer. The Apple II c and the Z80 were 8-bit computers for example and the 8 bit was introduced by the IBM System. MS Windows 7 came as a 64 bits version. MS Windows 10 has a 32 and a 64 bit version. New computers have a 64 bit processor. The 32 bit version can address 3.5 Gb RAM (32^2) memory and the 64 bit version up to 2TB (64^2) RAM memory. MS Windows 11 is 64 bits only.

---

[16] https://www.javatpoint.com/coa-main-memory

Attachment 1. Your own software and programs through the ages

Try to remember the software and programs you used through the decades and fill in this list for your own purpose. It helps to look for pictures online by typing the name of the software you are looking for in your search engine and select 'images'. How many have you used and can you remember?

name	supplier	purpose	year